SOLDIER!

PAUL BECK

ILLUSTRATED BY
RJ PALMER

DISCOVER 15 WARRIORS THROUGHOUT HISTORY

■ SCHOLASTIC

SOLDIER!

TABLE OF CONTENTS

INTRODUCTION

In this book you'll meet soldiers from all over the world, from more than 2,000 years ago to the present day. Some, like the knights of Europe or the samurai of Japan, were chosen for a military life from the time they were born. Others, like volunteer soldiers in the United States today, choose to become warriors on their own. Still others were conscripted, or drafted into their countries' armies in times of war. But no matter when, where, or how they become soldiers, all of them train to become experts at their weapons and learn to work as a team with their fellow soldiers. Trusting each other with their lives, they share the life of a warrior.

IMPERIAL ROMAN LEGIONARY

YEARS: 31 B.C.E.–284 C.E.

LOCATION: EUROPE, MIDDLE EAST, NORTH AFRICA

At its height, the Roman Empire stretched all the way across Western Europe, North Africa, and the Middle East. Rome conquered and held its territory by military force. Before 31 B.C.E., the army was assembled as needed each time there was a war. When Augustus Caesar became the first emperor, he turned the legions into a permanent professional force. Roman legionaries served for twenty-five years. Each soldier swore an oath called the *sacramentum*, in which he promised to follow all the emperor's commands, not to desert the army, and to be willing to die for Rome.

Helmet

Bronze or iron, lined with felt

SPECS

WEIGHT: 4.5–5 lb. (2–2.3 kg)	

A Roman legionary charged into battle carrying as much as 66 lb. (30 kg) of weapons and armor. On the march, his burden could top 100 lb. (45 kg), with the added weight of rations, cooking equipment, extra clothes, and digging tools.

Pugiō

Stabbing weapon for close-in fighting

SPECS

WEIGHT: 1 lb. (450 g)	
LENGTH: 8–13 in. (20–33 cm)	

Gladius

Cutting and thrusting weapon

SPECS

WEIGHT: 3.3 lb. (1.5 kg)	
LENGTH: 20 in. (51 cm)	

Caligae

Heavy sandals with hobnailed soles

IMPERIAL ROMAN LEGIONARY

WHAT THEY CARRIED

Scutum (shield) ««

Could be used for smashing an enemy as well as for defense

SPECS

WIDTH:	25 in. (64 cm)
LENGTH:	50 in. (127 cm)

Pilum (javelin) ««

Throwing weapon, able to pierce armor

Balteus (military belt) ««

The mark of a Roman soldier: a single or double belt with metal decorations

SPECS

WEIGHT:	4.4 lb. (2 kg) or more
LENGTH:	up to 5.5 ft. (168 cm)
RANGE:	up to 100 ft. (30 m)

TRAINING

It took four solid months of training to turn a raw recruit into a professional soldier. Training started with marching and maneuvers. Then recruits moved on to weapons training with wooden swords, shields, and javelins. These practice weapons were twice as heavy as the real ones, building up the soldiers' fighting strength and speed.

COMRADES IN ARMS

Each legionary was a member of an eight-man group called a *contubernium*. The soldiers of the contubernium lived together in the same room at the barracks and shared a tent in the field. They also cooked and ate together. The legionaries in a contubernium formed strong bonds of loyalty with one another and could count on their tent-mates in battle.

CONTUBERNIUM is Latin for "group that occupies a single tent."

Legionaries were responsible for carrying and preparing their own food. Meals in the fort or camp might include bread with some added vegetables or meat. On the march, soldiers carried hardtack (dry biscuits), which could be softened by cooking in hot water or fat.

VIKING

YEARS: 793-1066

LOCATION: EUROPE, RUSSIA, NORTH AMERICA

The Vikings were Scandinavians from the area that is now Denmark, Sweden, and Norway. Originally farmers and traders, they took up raiding by sea at the end of the 8th century. Residents of England, Ireland, and the coasts of Europe soon grew to fear the plundering raids of these fierce seafarers. Vikings lived in family groups and clans. Older clan members passed their fighting and battle knowledge on to younger ones.

Helmet

Iron with eye guards and chain mail neck protector

NO HORNS!

Viking battle helmets **DID NOT** have horns! Such decorations would only give enemies something to grab onto.

Mail shirt

Made of interlocking iron rings

Shield

Leather-covered wood with iron boss and iron or leather edging

SPECS
DIAMETER: 2 ft. (60 cm)

Sword

Early Viking swords were built for slashing. Later, more tapered swords could also be used for thrusting.

SPECS
WEIGHT: 2 lb. (900 g)
LENGTH: 3 ft. (91 cm)

Tunic

Leather boots

Swords were very expensive and likely owned only by wealthier Vikings.

VIKING

WHAT THEY CARRIED

Bearded Ax ≪

Older form of Viking battle ax

SPECS
LENGTH: 33 in. (83.8 cm)

Nestbaggin ≪

Leather pouch for carrying food

Spear ≪

Mainly a thrusting weapon, possibly also for throwing

SPECS
LENGTH: 6.5–10 ft. (2–3 m)

A WALL OF SHIELDS

A favorite Viking battle formation was the *skjaldborg*, or shield wall. The warriors would line up in a close pack, five or more men deep, with an interlocking wall of shields at the front.

Developed from the earlier bearded ax as blade styles became wider

LONGSHIPS

The Vikings were master shipwrights. They built their ships with overlapping boards, a method called *clinker-building*. A Viking ship was tall at the prow and stern, with a large steering oar on the starboard side. Warriors hung their shields in rows along the sides. Power came from both a sail and long oars pulled by a crew of as many as thirty. The sight of an approaching Viking longship was enough to strike terror into the heart of anyone who saw it pulling up to shore.

BERSERKR

Viking sagas tell of warriors called *berserkr*, who would go into a furious fit, charging into battle without armor and attacking the enemy with such crazy anger and strength that they couldn't be stopped.

SPECS
LENGTH: 55 in. (139.7 cm)

KNIGHT

YEARS: 1000–1500

LOCATION: EUROPE

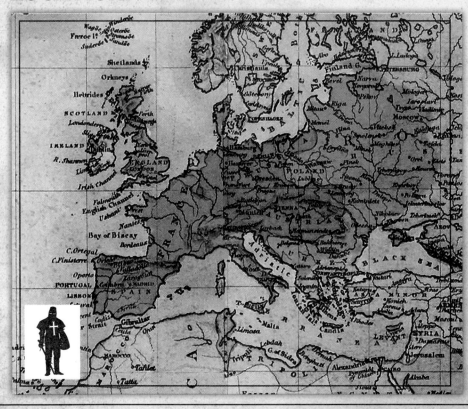

Medieval knights were noblemen who fought on horseback. They lived by a code of conduct called *chivalry*, which spelled out the rules for fighting battles and treating other people honorably. At the age of seven, boys who would become knights were sent to serve as pages in a nobleman's house. At the age of fourteen, a page could become a squire. A squire learned chivalry, fighting, and horsemanship. When he was fully trained and educated, a squire would be made a knight in a ceremony called *dubbing*.

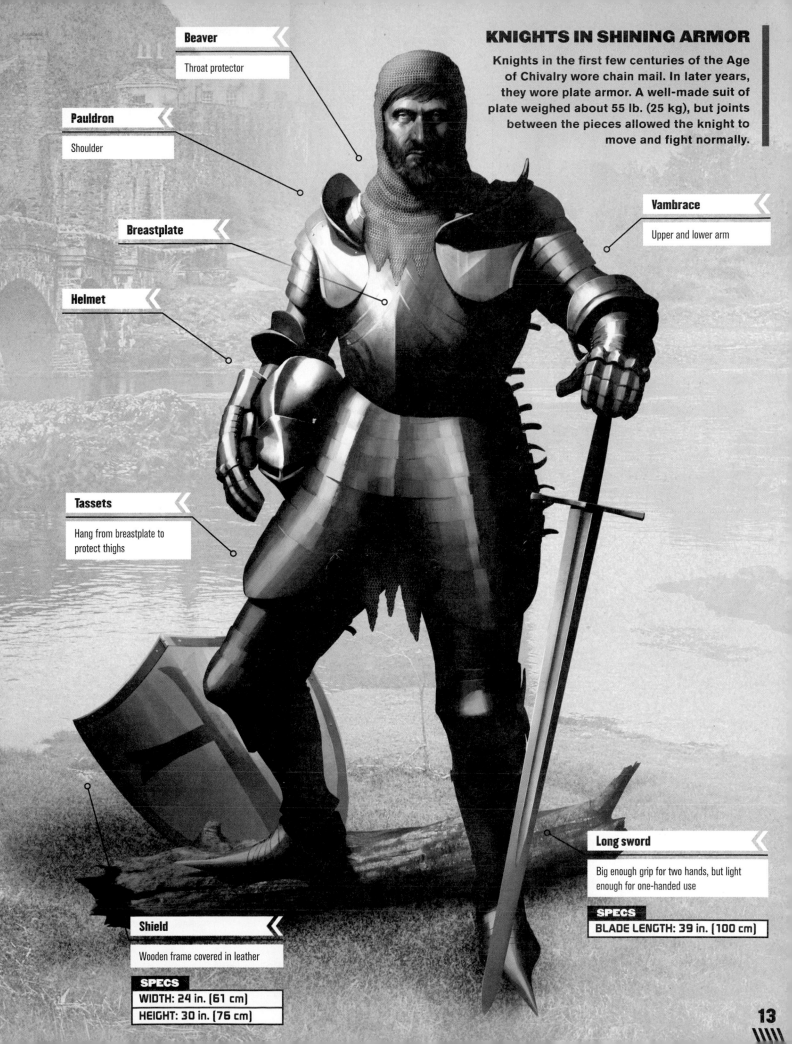

Beaver

Throat protector

Pauldron

Shoulder

Breastplate

Helmet

Tassets

Hang from breastplate to protect thighs

Shield

Wooden frame covered in leather

SPECS

WIDTH: 24 in. (61 cm)

HEIGHT: 30 in. (76 cm)

KNIGHTS IN SHINING ARMOR

Knights in the first few centuries of the Age of Chivalry wore chain mail. In later years, they wore plate armor. A well-made suit of plate weighed about 55 lb. (25 kg), but joints between the pieces allowed the knight to move and fight normally.

Vambrace

Upper and lower arm

Long sword

Big enough grip for two hands, but light enough for one-handed use

SPECS

BLADE LENGTH: 39 in. (100 cm)

SAMURAI

YEARS: 1180–1625

LOCATION: JAPAN

The samurai were military noblemen of medieval Japan, much like the knights of Europe. Samurai warriors served powerful lords known as *daimyo*, who themselves served the *shogun*, or military governor. Samurai without a daimyo hired themselves out as mercenaries, or *ronin*. Samurai lived, trained, and fought under a code of loyalty, honor, and martial arts mastery. This way of life later became known as *bushidō*, or the Way of the Warrior.

DRESSED FOR BATTLE

Samurai armor was made of iron plates, leather, or both. The armor pieces were fastened together with laces. The armor's metal plates were painted with colorful lacquer. Helmets often had crests and other decorations to identify the samurai who wore them. Some helmets featured face masks with grimacing mouths and bristling mustaches.

Kabuto

Helmet

Shikoro

Neck guard

Obi

Sash

Kusazuri

Armor plates to protect thighs

Suneate

Greaves, or leg armor

Do

Cuirass, or torso armor

Kote

Splint armor sleeves

Wakizashi

Companion sword

SPECS
BLADE LENGTH:
12–24 in. (30–60 cm)

Katana

Main sword

SPECS
BLADE LENGTH:
24–36 in. (61–91 cm)

Waraji

Straw sandals

A samurai on campaign carried all of his food, supplies, and equipment along with his armor and weapons.

SAMURAI

WHAT THEY CARRIED

DAISHO

A samurai's main weapons were a matched pair of swords called *daisho*, or "big and small." The *katana* was the longer sword, and the *wakizashi* was the shorter. Samurai swords are the finest-edged weapons ever made. The blades were forged and honed to razor sharpness by master swordsmiths.

Tanegashima «

Matchlock gun

TRAINING

Samurai started their training as young boys. They studied not only physical training but also subjects like music, art, and strategy games. Combat training started at age 13. Somewhere between the ages of 13 and 15, the young samurai officially became a warrior in a ceremony called *genpuku*. Samurai fought their first battles as teenagers.

Yari (lance)

Thrusting weapon, not thrown

Samurai got ahead by being noticed for their deeds in battle. Warriors made themselves recognizable with distinctive, decorated armor.

★

YUMI

In the earliest days of the samurai, the bow, or *yumi*, was the most important weapon. The 7–9 ft. (2–2.7 m), wood and bamboo laminated weapon had a range of up to 415 yds. (380 m), or more than four football fields.

Aikuchi (dagger)

For close combat

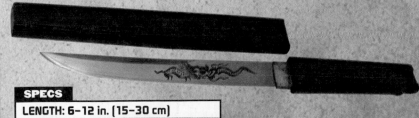

SPECS
LENGTH: 3.3–10 ft. (1–3 m)

SPECS
LENGTH: 6–12 in. (15–30 cm)

WARRIOR

NAPOLEONIC SOLDIER

YEARS: 1796–1815

LOCATION: EUROPE

At the beginning of the 1800s, the French general Napoleon Bonaparte tried to conquer all of Europe. At its biggest, Napoleon's Grand Army had more than 600,000 soldiers from all of the countries in his empire. But Napoleon's plans were foiled. In 1812, his army was destroyed when he tried to invade Russia. He assembled his forces again in 1815, but was defeated for good at the Battle of Waterloo, in what is now Belgium.

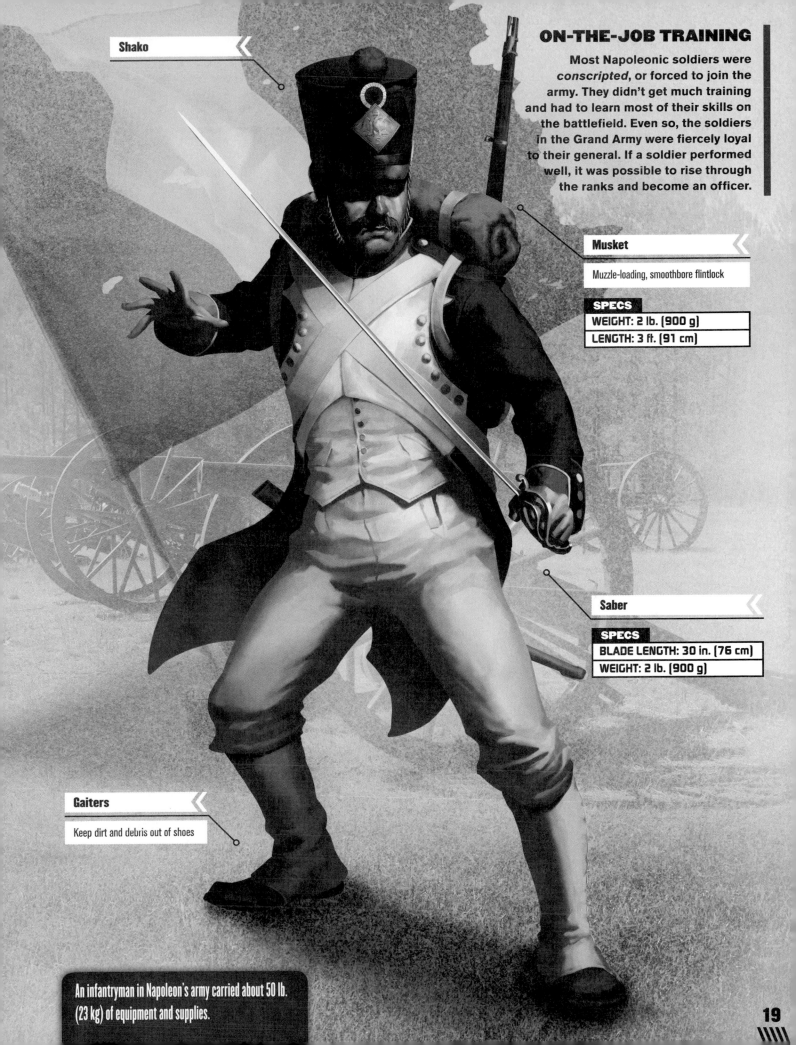

Shako

ON-THE-JOB TRAINING

Most Napoleonic soldiers were *conscripted*, or forced to join the army. They didn't get much training and had to learn most of their skills on the battlefield. Even so, the soldiers in the Grand Army were fiercely loyal to their general. If a soldier performed well, it was possible to rise through the ranks and become an officer.

Musket

Muzzle-loading, smoothbore flintlock

SPECS
WEIGHT: 2 lb. (900 g)
LENGTH: 3 ft. (91 cm)

Saber

SPECS
BLADE LENGTH: 30 in. (76 cm)
WEIGHT: 2 lb. (900 g)

Gaiters

Keep dirt and debris out of shoes

An infantryman in Napoleon's army carried about 50 lb. (23 kg) of equipment and supplies.

CIVIL WAR UNION SOLDIER

YEARS: 1861–1865

LOCATION: UNITED STATES

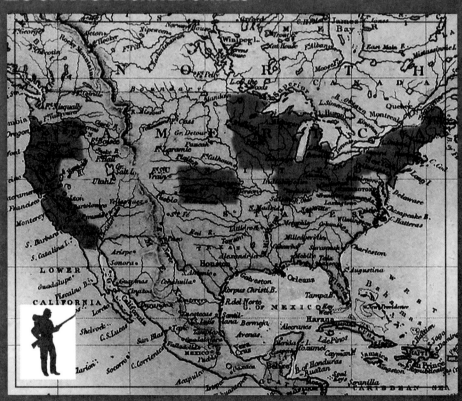

At the start of the American Civil War, patriotic Northerners rushed to volunteer for the U.S. Army. Most people expected the war to be over quickly. Many volunteers thought life as a soldier would be heroic and adventurous. Instead, the war lasted four years, and army life turned out to be difficult, unpleasant, and very dangerous.

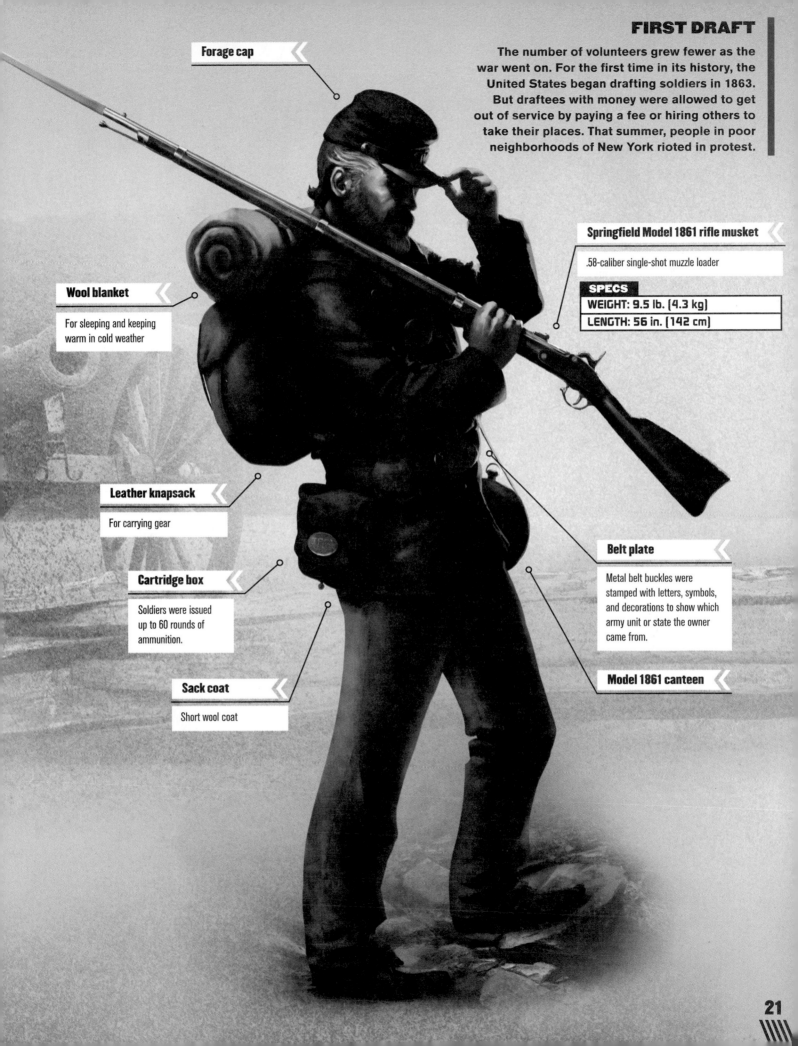

Forage cap «

The number of volunteers grew fewer as the war went on. For the first time in its history, the United States began drafting soldiers in 1863. But draftees with money were allowed to get out of service by paying a fee or hiring others to take their places. That summer, people in poor neighborhoods of New York rioted in protest.

Springfield Model 1861 rifle musket «

.58-caliber single-shot muzzle loader

SPECS
WEIGHT: 9.5 lb. (4.3 kg)
LENGTH: 56 in. (142 cm)

Wool blanket «

For sleeping and keeping warm in cold weather

Leather knapsack «

For carrying gear

Belt plate «

Metal belt buckles were stamped with letters, symbols, and decorations to show which army unit or state the owner came from.

Cartridge box «

Soldiers were issued up to 60 rounds of ammunition.

Model 1861 canteen «

Sack coat «

Short wool coat

CIVIL WAR UNION SOLDIER

WHAT THEY CARRIED

HAND GRENADES

The hand grenade was a new invention at the time of the Civil War. Grenades had fuses that detonated them on impact. They were often more dangerous to the soldier throwing them than to the person they were thrown at.

RIFLING

Unlike a smoothbore gun, a rifle has a twisting pattern of grooves cut into the inside of the barrel. Called *rifling*, the grooves cause the bullet to spin as it leaves the barrel. The spin makes the bullet travel straighter and farther. Civil War soldiers used both muzzle-loading rifles (muskets) and breech-loading rifles.

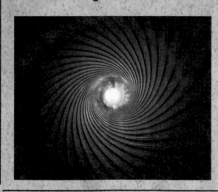

Bayonet

Allows muskets or other long guns to be used as a thrusting weapon

Ramrod

Fits in holder below barrel

Spencer rifle

.52-caliber breech-loading, repeating rifle with a 7-shot magazine

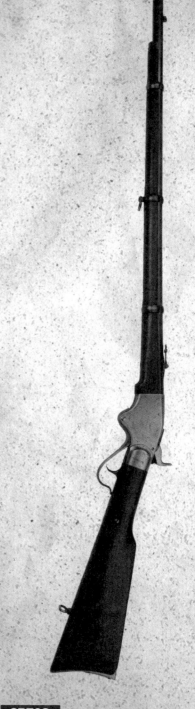

SPECS	
WEIGHT:	10 lb. (4.5 kg)
LENGTH:	47 in. (119 cm)

Colt Model 1848 revolver

.44-caliber, 6-shot

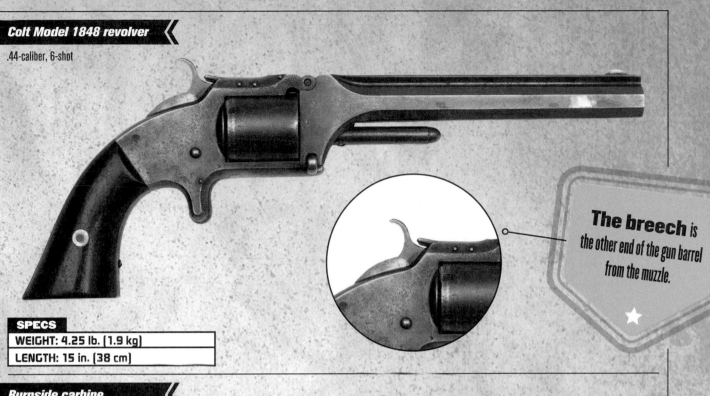

SPECS

WEIGHT: 4.25 lb. (1.9 kg)	
LENGTH: 15 in. (38 cm)	

The breech is the other end of the gun barrel from the muzzle.

★

Burnside carbine

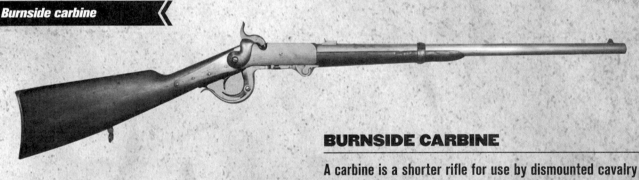

SPECS

WEIGHT: 7 lb. (3.2 kg)	
LENGTH: 39.5 in. (100 cm)	

BURNSIDE CARBINE

A carbine is a shorter rifle for use by dismounted cavalry soldiers. The Burnside carbine was designed by General Ambrose Burnside, whose facial hair style gave us the word "sideburns."

JAW-BREAKERS

Soldiers' main food on the march was hardtack—thick wheat crackers baked and dried nearly as hard as rocks. The men called the crackers names like "jaw-breakers" and "teeth-dullers." Soaking hardtack in water or cooking it in stew made it easier to eat. Soldiers' rations also included coffee and sugar, along with whatever meat and other foods were available.

Very few men of the time knew how to cook, so meals could be truly terrible. Eventually the army began training cooks—one for every 100-soldier company.

★

CIVIL WAR CONFEDERATE SOLDIER

YEARS: 1861–1865

LOCATION: UNITED STATES

A Confederate soldier's life was one of shortage and scrounging. The soldiers had weapons and ammunition, but other equipment and supplies were scarce. They often had to find food, clothing, and tools wherever they could, including stealing or scavenging Union Army supplies.

NOT-SO-UNIFORM UNIFORMS

At the beginning of the war, the Confederacy hadn't yet created a uniform for its army. Instead, soldiers had the different uniforms of their state or local militias. Even after regular army uniforms were created, they weren't always the familiar Confederate gray. Some were brown, tan, and, in the early days, even blue.

Kepi

Low-style cap chosen because tall shakos made soldiers more visible targets

Shell jacket

Cartridge box

Regulation issue was 40 cartridges

Enfield Pattern 1853 rifle musket

Imported British Muzzle-loading rifle .58-caliber, single-shot

SPECS

WEIGHT: 9.5 lb. (4.3 kg)

LENGTH: 55 in. (140 cm)

Wood canteen

Wool trousers

Shoes

Shoes were occasionally in such short supply that some soldiers had to march barefoot. Legend has it that the Battle of Gettysburg was sparked by a Confederate foray to get a supply of shoes.

The North already had a supply of weapons for its army, as well as factories for making more. The Confederacy didn't have enough factories to produce all the guns they needed. They imported many weapons from other countries such as England and France. Confederate soldiers also used captured Union weapons and equipment.

APACHE WARRIOR

YEARS: 1861–1886

LOCATION: SOUTHWEST UNITED STATES

The Apache are a Native American people from the southwestern United States and northern Mexico. From the earliest time of European contact, the Apache had a reputation as fierce warriors.

In the 1800s, settlers, prospectors, and military forces from the United States and Mexico began taking over Apache lands. After being treated badly and in some cases attacked or killed by these intruders, a group of Apache warriors fought a guerrilla resistance war against the United States.

Traditional headband

Cloth shirt and vest

European-American style

TRADITIONAL...

Before the Apache adopted guns, their traditional weapons included the bow and arrow, lance, and sling. Bows were made of wood strengthened by layers of animal sinew. Arrow points were stone, bone, or iron.

...AND MODERN

Along with the Springfield rifle, Apache warriors of the 1800s wielded weapons such as the Winchester Model 1873 repeating rifle and the Colt Model 1873 revolver.

Springfield Model 1873 "trap-door" rifle

Breech-loading rifle
.45-caliber, single-shot

SPECS
LENGTH: 52 in. (132 cm)

Moccasins

Tall boot-style leather shoes

Cloth breeches

European-American style

Geronimo, or Goyathlay ("One Who Yawns"), is the most famous Apache warrior. In 1886, he was the leader of the last armed Native American resistance to surrender to the U.S. government.

WWI GERMAN INFANTRYMAN

YEARS: 1914–1918

LOCATION: EUROPE AND MIDDLE EAST

When German soldiers went to war in August 1914, they believed they were defending their country. Germany had declared war on France, claiming that the French were encroaching on German territory. What the common soldiers didn't know was that their leaders were actually planning to invade and take over most of Europe.

Pickelhaube

Spiked leather helmet

Halfway through the war the German army switched to a new helmet made of steel, called the *Stahlhelm*.

Backpack

Cloth with leather flap

Cartridge pouches

Breadbag

For food rations

Stick grenade

Nicknamed "potato masher"

REQUIRED SERVICE

All German men were required to serve in the military from age seventeen to age forty-five. Before the war, the first three years of service were in the *Landsturm*, similar to the National Guard in the United States. Once the war began, all men from seventeen to twenty-two went into the regular army.

Gas mask in case

Protection from chemical weapons

Greatcoat

Mauser Gewehr 98 rifle

Bolt-action rifle
7.92mm, 5-round magazine

SPECS

WEIGHT: 9 lb. (4.1 kg)
LENGTH: 49 in. (124 cm)

Meals in the German army included bread; fresh, frozen, or canned meat; potatoes or vegetables; and coffee or tea. As the war went on and supplies grew short, the meat ration was made smaller, and on one day per week there was no meat at all.

WWI AMERICAN EXPEDITIONARY FORCES SOLDIER

YEARS: 1917–1918

LOCATION: EUROPE AND MIDDLE EAST

World War I had been raging in Europe for nearly three years by the time the United States entered the conflict. But the U.S. Army was the smallest it had been since the Civil War. It needed lots of new recruits. Volunteers rushed to sign up, but there weren't enough, and the government began drafting soldiers. All men aged twenty-one to thirty-one had to register. If drafted, they had to serve until the war was over.

M1917 helmet

First U.S. Army helmet made of steel

Bedroll

DOUGHBOYS

American soldiers in World War I were known as doughboys. Nobody knows where the nickname came from, but it dates back to the Civil War or earlier. The French were *poilu* ("hairy ones," named for their beards and mustaches). The British were called Tommies.

M1903 Springfield rifle

Bolt-action, 5-round magazine
.30-caliber

SPECS
WEIGHT: 8.8 lb. (4 kg)
LENGTH: 43 in. (109 cm)

M1910/14 cartridge belt

With 60 rounds of ammunition

1917 "drab" uniform

Color varied from brown to olive green

Puttees

Strips of cloth wound around legs for support and to keep mud out of boots

Boots

Hobnailed soles for traction

By the end of the war, 2.1 million U.S. soldiers were in Europe.

WWI AMERICAN EXPEDITIONARY FORCES SOLDIER

WHAT THEY CARRIED

Vickers machine gun

British-made heavy machine gun
.303-caliber, 250-round ammunition
belt, 500 rounds per minute

SPECS	
WEIGHT: 42 lb. (19 kg)	
LENGTH: 42 in. (107 cm)	
TRIPOD WEIGHT: 56 lb. (25 kg)	

Winchester Model 1897

Pump-action shotgun for trench warfare
12-gauge, 5-round magazine

SPECS	
WEIGHT: 8 lb. (3.6 kg)	
LENGTH: 39 in. (100 cm)	

M1915 Chauchat automatic rifle

French-made light machine 8mm gun, 20-round
magazine, 250 rounds per minute

SPECS	
WEIGHT: 22 lb. (10 kg)	
LENGTH: 45 in. (114 cm)	

Trench knife

Guard acts as brass knuckles
for punching

M1906 Bayonet

Gas mask
Protection against chemical gas attacks

Entrenching tool
Shovel for digging trenches

TRAINING

The United States needed to build up a large army in a hurry. Most doughboys were conscripts (draftees) with no military experience. They went through basic training in the United States. Afterward, they were rushed by ship to France, where they were trained in trench warfare before being sent into battle.

IN THE TRENCHES

World War I was fought using trench warfare, in which soldiers dug deep trenches to protect themselves from enemy guns and artillery. The trenches were very unpleasant places to be, especially in bad weather, but troops were rotated in and out of trench positions so they wouldn't have to spend too much time there.

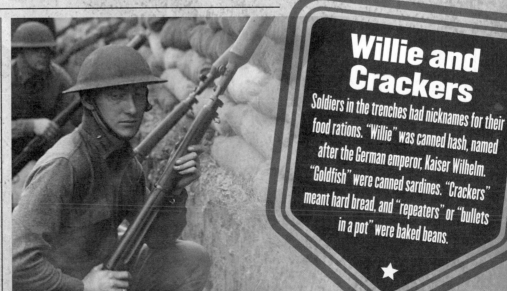

Willie and Crackers

Soldiers in the trenches had nicknames for their food rations. "Willie" was canned hash, named after the German emperor, Kaiser Wilhelm. "Goldfish" were canned sardines. "Crackers" meant hard bread, and "repeaters" or "bullets in a pot" were baked beans.

WWII ROYAL AIR FORCE AIR GUNNER

YEARS: 1939–1945

LOCATION: WESTERN EUROPE

The bombers of Britain's Royal Air Force flew missions high above German territory. Along with a fighter escort, the bombers had their own guns to defend themselves against enemy attacks. RAF air gunners manned their guns inside glass-covered turrets. The turrets gave them all-around visibility, but they also exposed the gunners to deadly enemy fire.

Type B helmet

Leather with padded pouches for earphones

Goggles

Tinted lenses known as "windows" cut glare and protected the gunner's eyes in case of a break or leak in the turret glass.

RAF bombers flew at high altitudes, where the temperature could get as low as -45° F (-43° C). Gun turrets weren't heated, so air gunners needed flying suits, gloves, and boots that would keep them warm.

Oxygen mask

With microphone for communication

Irvin flying suit

Made of fleece-lined sheepskin for warmth

Life jacket

Parachute

Boots

Sheepskin-lined and heated by chemical heating pads

Air crews wore life jackets and parachutes at all times during a mission in case they had to bail out over land or water.

WWII U.S. ARMY FIELD COMBAT SOLDIER

YEARS: 1941–1945

LOCATION: AFRICA, EUROPE, ASIA, AND THE PACIFIC

The American soldiers who fought in World War II came from all walks of life. Some were in the army before the war, but many volunteered after the Japanese attack on Pearl Harbor in 1941. They left their jobs and families and went through training to learn how to use weapons and master the other special skills they would need in battle, such as working radio equipment, driving tanks, or even flying airplanes.

HEAVY LOAD

A U.S. Army field combat soldier carried an average of 60 lb. (27 kg) of weapons and equipment. That's about the weight of an eight-year-old kid!

Field pack

M1 helmet

Steel with padded fiber lining

M1943 field jacket

Cotton cloth, wind- and water-resistant

M1943 wool trousers

M1 Garand rifle

Semiautomatic rifle
.30-caliber, 8-round magazine

SPECS
WEIGHT: 9.5 lb. (4.3 kg)
LENGTH: 44 in. (112 cm)

M1943 combat boots

When a soldier fired the M1 rifle, expanding gas from the shell cocked the gun, loaded a new round, and ejected the fired cartridge. The rifle fired repeated shots as fast as the soldier could pull the trigger.

WWII U.S. ARMY FIELD COMBAT SOLDIER

WHAT THEY CARRIED

M1 Thompson submachine gun

"Tommy gun"
.45-caliber, 20-, 30-, or 50-round magazine

SPECS

WEIGHT: 10.75 lb. (4.9 kg)	
LENGTH: 34 in. (86 cm)	

Mess kit

Known as a "meat can"

Gas mask

Canteen

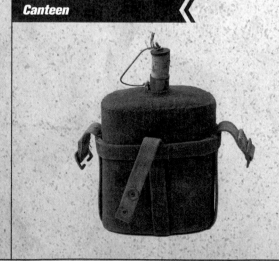

LIVING OUT OF A PACK

In their packs, combat soldiers carried everything they needed to eat, sleep, and protect themselves. The standard gear for all soldiers included weapons and ammunition, goggles, a rain poncho, wool sleeping bag, shovel to dig trenches, gas mask, and helmet. Radio technicians and medics had even more gear to carry.

FORWARD MARCH!

All soldiers spent thirteen weeks in basic training before shipping out. There they learned to use weapons, work as a unit (including hours and hours of marching), and form strong friendships with their fellow soldiers.

M1 Carbine

Shorter version of the M1 rifle
.30 caliber, 15-round magazine

SPECS

WEIGHT: 5.2 lb. (2.4 kg)	
LENGTH: 36 in. (91 cm)	

M1903 Springfield rifle

Bolt-action sniper rifle
.30-caliber, 5-round magazine

SPECS

WEIGHT: 8.8 lb. (4 kg)	
LENGTH: 43 in. (109 cm)	

Mk 2 "pineapple" grenade

Fragmentation grenade

M1911A1 Colt semiautomatic pistol

.45-caliber, 7-round magazine

SPECS

WEIGHT: 2.4 lb. (1.1 kg)	
LENGTH: 8.25 in. (21 cm)	

WWII IMPERIAL JAPANESE ARMY SOLDIER

YEARS: 1941–1945

LOCATION: THE PACIFIC

The soldiers of the Imperial Japanese Army were fierce fighters. They and their commanders believed that *seishin*, or strength of will, would let them triumph even when outnumbered or facing an enemy with better weapons and equipment. They were taught that it was a disgrace to surrender or be captured, and it was better to die for their emperor.

Field cap (with Sun curtain)

Sun curtain protects neck

HOT WEATHER GEAR

The Japanese Army fought most of its WWII battles in tropical areas. They wore lightweight uniforms and even shorts in the summer. But carrying pounds and pounds of gear and weapons through the jungle was still punishingly hot work.

Arisaka Type 99 "short" rifle

Short version, better for jungle fighting
Bolt-action 7.7mm, 5-round magazine

SPECS
WEIGHT: 8.5 lb. (3.9 kg)
LENGTH: 44 in. (112 cm)

Water purification kit

Tube with filter for filling canteen

Ammunition pouch

Puttees

Strips of cloth support and protect lower legs

Tabi shoes

Made of canvas and rubber, with separate big toe

The tropical jungle climate caused uniforms to break down and wear out quickly. As more and more of the army's supply lines got cut during the war, it got harder for soldiers to get replacements. They had to make do with whatever clothes they could make or find. Once, Japanese soldiers in New Guinea had to dress in rice bags after their uniforms had completely disintegrated.

VIETNAM WAR U.S. MARINE RIFLEMAN

YEARS: 1965–1975

LOCATION: SOUTH VIETNAM

Marines are soldiers of the sea. Their main mission is attacking land positions from the water. That means there's no easy way to retreat. Marine training was (and still is) much harder and more intense than that of other military branches. New recruits first went through ten weeks of basic training, in which they learned close-order drill marching, marksmanship, first aid, knife and bayonet fighting, and other skills. After basic training, marines went on to an Infantry Training Regiment, which was even tougher than boot camp.

M1 helmet with camouflage cover

Used by soldiers since WWII

SURVIVING IN THE JUNGLE

Marines in Vietnam were supposed to carry about 50 lb. (23 kg) of weapons and equipment. But they knew that they wouldn't have anything they didn't carry themselves, so they often had as much as 80 or even 100 lb. (36 to 45 kg) of gear.

Ka-Bar fighting knife

M26 fragmentation grenade

Vietnam-era grenades were much more powerful than the ones from WWII

M79 grenade launcher

Fires one 40mm high-explosive round

SPECS

RANGE:	1,230 ft. (375 m)
WEIGHT:	5.9 lb. (2.7 kg)
LENGTH:	29 in. (74 cm)

M55 body armor

Not bulletproof, but meant to protect the soldier from flying shrapnel

M14 rifle

Gas-operated semiautomatic rifle

SPECS

WEIGHT:	9.2 lb. (4.2 kg)
LENGTH:	44 in. (112 cm)

Jungle combat boots

Made of nylon and leather

The rifle is the marine's main weapon. During the Vietnam War, the M14 was replaced by the M16, which is still in use today.

U.S. NAVY SEAL

YEARS: 1962–PRESENT DAY

LOCATION: WORLDWIDE

SEALs are the U.S. Navy's special forces. Their name stands for SEa, Air, Land, where these warriors perform their missions. Less than 1 percent of the people in the Navy are SEALs.

A SEAL's gear and weapons depend on his particular mission. It might involve demolition, rescuing prisoners or soldiers, reconnaissance in enemy countries, an anti-terrorism mission, or other special activities.

Night vision goggles

TOUGH COMPETITION

Because Navy SEALs only take the best of the best, you have to pass a tough physical screening test (PST) even to be considered. Candidates compete for high scores in swimming, push-ups, curl-ups, pull-ups, and running.

Body armor

Vest holds bullet-stopping armor plates

Tactical backpack

For carrying essential equipment

Radio communications equipment

M16 rifle with night vision scope and laser aiming system

Gas-operated assault rifle
5.56mm, 20-, 30-, or 100-round magazine

SPECS

WEIGHT: 7.18 lb. (3.3 kg)	
LENGTH: 39 in. (100 cm)	

Knee pads

U.S. NAVY SEAL

WHAT THEY CARRY

M14 sniper rifle

Gas-operated semiautomatic rifle
7.62mm, 20-round magazine

SPECS

WEIGHT: 9.2 lb. (4.2 kg)	
LENGTH: 44 in. (112 cm)	

M203 grenade launcher

Attaches to bottom of rifle barrel,
fires one 40mm high-explosive round

SPECS

WEIGHT: 3 lb. (1.4 kg)	
LENGTH: 15 in. (38 cm)	

Heckler & Koch P7M13 pistol

Semiautomatic pistol
9mm, 8-round magazine

SPECS

WEIGHT: 1.9 lb. (862 g)	
LENGTH: 6.9 in. (17.5 cm)	

Stinger antiaircraft missile launcher

Fires surface-to-air missle
Range: 5 mi. (8km)

SPECS

WEIGHT: 33.5 lb. (15.2 kg)	
LENGTH: 60 in. (152 cm)	

UNDERWATER BREATHING APPARATUS

Navy SEAL history goes back to the underwater demolition frogmen of WWII. Underwater assault is still a big part of their mission.

SEALs use two different kinds of UBA, or underwater breathing apparatus:

- **Open-circuit UBA** is regular scuba gear, with tanks of compressed air. When the SEAL breathes out, the air escapes as bubbles in the water.

- **Closed-circuit UBA** recycles the gas. It never leaves the tanks, so there are no bubbles to give away the SEAL's location to the enemy. One type of closed circuit UBA uses pure oxygen, but it can only be used for shallow dives without endangering the diver. The other uses a mix of air and oxygen, so the diver can go deeper.

BECOMING A SEAL

Navy sailors who want to become SEALs go through an intense training called BUD/S, or Basic Underwater Demolition/SEAL. It starts with five solid weeks of 4 mi. (6.4 km) runs, 2 mi. (3.2 km) swims, boat skill training, and "Hell Week," in which would-be SEALs go for five and a half days of training exercises with a *total* of only four hours of sleep. Those who survive Hell Week go on to eight weeks of dive training, nine weeks of land warfare training, and another six to twelve months of advanced training in such skills as parachute jumping and medical training.

SOLDIER!

This edition published by Scholastic Inc., 557 Broadway, New York, NY 10012 by arrangement with becker&mayer! LLC. Scholastic and associated logos are trademarks and/or registered trademarks of Scholastic Inc.

Scholastic Inc., New York, NY

Produced by becker&mayer!, LLC.
11120 NE 33rd Place, Suite 101
Bellevue, WA 98004
www.beckermayer.com

ISBN: 978-0-545-93161-8

Author: Paul Beck
Designer: Sam Dawson
Illustrator: RJ Palmer
Editor: Dana Youlin
Photo researcher: Donna Metcalf
Production coordinator: Tom Miller

IMAGE CREDITS:
Every effort has been made to trace copyright holders. If any unintended omissions have been made, becker&mayer! would be pleased to add appropriate acknowledgements in future editions. Cover: Military fabric pattern ©WitthayaP/Shutterstock Digital camouflage texture ©Casper1774 Studio/Shutterstock.
Page 1: Rust backgrounds ©ilolab/Shutterstock; Pages 2-3: US army camouflage fabric texture background ©Casper1774 Studio/Shutterstock; World map ©Bardocz Peter/Shutterstock; Page 5: Ruins (dungeons) of the colosseum in in North Africa. El Jem, Tunisia. UNESCO ©Marques/Shutterstock; Pages 6-7: Roman shield ©Photosampler/Shutterstock; Roman soldier ©meunierd/Shutterstock; Roman Legionary ©Lagui/Shutterstock; Steel pilum ©Viktorija Reuta/Shutterstock; Roman Centurion ©standby/iStock; Roman soldiers reenactment ©meunierd/Shutterstock; Roman Cooking ©verityjohnson/Shutterstock; Pages 10-11: Medieval axe ©CreativeHQ/Shutterstock; Viking leather bag ©Ryszard Filipowicz/Shutterstock; Antique spearhead ©My name is boy/Shutterstock; Viking Sailor Shields ©Holger Leue/ Getty Images; Medieval Barbarian or Viking vintage axe ©CreativeHQ/Shutterstock; Viking Ship Replica, Pegwell Bay, Thanet, Kent, UK ©Alan Gordine/Shutterstock; Wolin Viking Festival ©ewg3D/iStock; Pages 12-13: Rusted body armor ©Nanisimova/Shutterstock; Eilean Donan Castle in the Highlands of Scotland ©JeniFoto/Shutterstock; Page 15: Summer in bamboo forest ©YuryZap/Shutterstock; Pages 16-17 Katana swords ©Janice Adlam/Shutterstock; Samurai Train for Rebellion ©Ivy Close Images / Alamy Stock Photo; A matchlock teppo ©INTERFOTO / Alamy Stock Photo; Yari blade ©INTERFOTO / Alamy Stock Photo; Kyudo - modern Japanese martial art. ©KUCO/Shutterstock; Japanese knife ©Yan Vugenfirer/Shutterstock; Page 19 A battery of civil war cannon lined up ©Denton Rumsey/Shutterstock; French Flag ©Mr Doomits/Shutterstock; Page 21: Civil War era cannon overlooks Kennesaw ©Rob Hainer/Shutterstock; Pages 22-23: Round Metal Bomb with Fuse ©Mega Pixel/Shutterstock; 18th century cannonball ©Mediagram/Shutterstock; Bayonet ©Militarist/Shutterstock; Infantry Spencer rifle M 1860 © INTERFOTO / Alamy Stock Photo; Inside view of a tank barrel ©Varchyk/Shutterstock; Pattern pistol built in the original percussion ©INTERFOTO / Alamy Stock Photo; Antique revolver ©Robert B. Miller/Shutterstock; American Civil War Weapons ©Orlando/ Stringer/ Getty Images; Detail of Civil War armament on display in an encampment ©Jim Parkin/Shutterstock; Page 25: Old building in full flaming inferno, and a firefighter fighting the flames ©Ufulum/Shutterstock; Page 26: Silhouettes of American Indians on horseback ©Makc/Shutterstock; Page 27: Blooming Palo Verde trees under a moody sky in the Sonoran Desert near Phoenix, Arizona ©Dave Morgan/Shutterstock; Pages 28-29: WWI german medal Iron Cross ©Militarist/Shutterstock; WWI trench Belgium Flanders ©Willequet Manuel/Shutterstock; Page 31: Trench of death WWI Belgium Flanders Fields ©Willequet Manuel/Shutterstock; Pages 32-33: Vickers-Berthier Mk.3 ©Marafona/Shutterstock; Winchester trench gun © INTERFOTO / Alamy Stock Photo; Auto rifle French-made ©INTERFOTO / Alamy Stock Photo; Great War Trench Knife/Model 1918 © a katz/Shutterstock; WWI Helmet and Bayonet ©Steve Bower/Shutterstock; Doughboys wear gas masks in the trenches during WWI ©Everett Historical/Shutterstock; Training camp, Image Courtesy of The U.S National Archives; infantry small shovel © Militarist/Shutterstock; U.S. Army soldier, probably in training in 1917-18 ©Everett Historical/Shutterstock; Pages 34-35: Natural brown leather texture ©Hitdelight/Shutterstock; Tied down British Supermarine Spifire in front of shack ©Dennis Steen/Shutterstock; Pages 38-39: WW2 British Army Equipment ©Dennis Steen/Shutterstock; Vintage canteen and portable cooking equipment, early 1900s. ©Jamie Roach/Shutterstock; old gas mask ©CreativeHQ/Shutterstock; Vintage military canteen ©Jamie Roach/Shutterstock; Second Army Tennessee Maneuvers. Image Courtesy of Sgt. J. A. Grant/ The U.S. National Archives; Semi-automatic M1 Carbine ©Stocktrek Images, Inc. / Alamy Stock Photo; Springfield rifle from early 1900's ©CreativeHQ/Shutterstock; Grenade frag explosive mk2 ©Casper1774 Studio/Shutterstock; Colt government m1911 ©Militarist/Shutterstock; Page 41: The scenic desert beach of the little Ee Island in the Aitutaki atoll, Cook Islands, South Pacific. ©Fabio Lamanna/Shutterstock; Page 43: Subtropical forest in Nepal ©Quick Shot/Shutterstock; Page 44: Military dog tags ©Maria Dryfhout/Shutterstock; Pages 46-47: M14 sniper rifle ©Militarist/Shutterstock; M16 rifle with an M203 grenade launcher ©Militarist/Shutterstock; weapon collection ©igorlale/Shutterstock; 2nd Low Altitude Air Defense Battalion Stinger Fire Exercise, Image Courtesy of U.S. Marine Corps/ Cpl. Allison Herman; GTMO's Navy Divers, Image Courtesy of U.S. Marine Corps/Chief Petty Officer Bill Mesta; U.S. Navy SEALs train, Image Courtesy of U.S. Marine Corps/Petty Officer 3rd Class Adam Henderson.
Used throughout: World map ©RTimages/Shutterstock; Bamboo fence ©somchaiP/Shutterstock; Set of four straight feathers ©Potapov Alexander/Shutterstock; Light green canvas texture ©Cristian Gusa/Shutterstock; Gold star ©Kunkie99/Shutterstock; Vintage Template ©MaxyM/Shutterstock; Set of military and armed forces badges and labels logo ©Mike McDonald/Shutterstock; Red and white fur ©homydesign/Shutterstock; Ancient and modern warriors silhouettes set ©vadimmmus/Shutterstock; Rust backgrounds ©ilolab/Shutterstock